Why Salt the Peanuts?

SAYINGS OF THE

5¢ PSYCHIATRIST

Benjamin Weininger

and Henry Rabin

Cover illustration and foreword

by Charles Schulz

The Guild of Tutors Press

Compiled by Richard Ogust.
Designed by Paul O. Proehl.

Photograph of Dr. Weininger by Julian Wasser.
Photograph of Dr. Rabin by Rothschild, Los Angeles.

Library of Congress Catalog Number: 78-75230

ISBN: 89615-020-8

FOREWORD

It is probably quite safe to say that all of us had a parent, or at least a grandparent, who spouted aphorisms. These little bits of truths have probably helped most of us to grow up and get wherever it was we had planned to go. My favorite was one that I recall my grandmother saying in times of distress. She had had nine children and certainly more than her share of trouble. "When children are small, they step on your toes, and when they grow up, they step on your heart." My grandmother had learned a lot and had learned it the hard way. Aphorisms, of course, are very short, like comic strips. If I have a reader for more than sixteen seconds a day, it is a rare occasion. Charlie Brown complained one morning after listening to Lucy that he felt covered with aphorisms. Linus suggested, "Maybe you need to be sprayed." Nothing in this world would be more foolish than a long introduction to a book of aphorisms. I must say, however, that this collection contains enough truths to make up for any that your grandmother might have forgotten.

Charles M. Schulz

DR. BEN'S INTRODUCTION

In 1970, as part of a project to publicize the need for more low-cost counseling, I had a booth built along the lines of that of the "Peanuts" comic strip created by that skillful observer of the human comedy, Charles Schulz. And in the spirit of Christmas I sat for ten days in the booth on the street in front of the Southern California Counseling Center, of which I am co-founder. The Center's fees at that time ranged from nothing to ten dollars per week. I had intended to hold forth at the booth only once, but my friend, Milton Taubman, persuaded me to continue the booth on a yearly basis before Christmas, which we did in different parts of Los Angeles. People of all ages came to the booth, from aged 9 to their late 70's.

These aphorisms are not a direct result of what we did in the booth. There I did regular counseling, the same as I would do in my office when brief psychotherapy was indicated. I've learned that when I do brief psychotherapy, I take off my watch. I'm completely relaxed, unhurried, and my intention is clearer. This arouses greater intensity in the patient, and frequently a breakthrough in one area of life is made. I discuss in these situations only one problem that is presented, and associations related to the problem. And when that is finished, the interview is over.

To mention two examples: A middle-aged man came by who seemed very much depressed. He was already undergoing therapy, for a month ago his wife of 30 years had left him for a wealthier man, and he told me he had a strong drive to end his life. He had two daughters. When I asked what they felt about this, he said that he hadn't told his daughters or any of his friends about it yet. I suggested that probably he wanted to kill himself, not because his wife left him, but because he was keeping it a secret. He gave me a nickel and thanked me.

Another man in his thirties said to me that he was honest and told people what he thought and consequently he drove his friends away. I responded, "It is important to learn to be honest with oneself and tactful with others."

The aphoristic style of this book was suggested to me by my friend and associate, Henry Rabin. We have had many discussions over the years about psychology and political events. We have learned from each other and tried a variety of ways of putting our insights into a form that others might benefit from our combined digested life experiences. The aphoristic style appealed to both of us. We both think that way, and it's hard to tell which are his aphorisms and which are mine. When I read too many aphorisms at a time, I find them interesting, but they pass through me, and I forget them. So my advice about reading this book is, read a few pages at a time, or even just a page. When some line of thought is important to me, I take some time out to think about it and sometimes discuss it with a friend.

I would like to express my appreciation to Jim Byers for his encouragement, to Sylvia Brickley for her help and valuable suggestions, and to Richard Ogust for his assitance in compiling the aphorisms. Frances Christian typed several successive versions, and for her help and patience I am grateful.

I hope you enjoy reading and learning from some of them as I enjoyed having them pop into my mind.

Benjamin Weininger

DR. RABIN'S INTRODUCTION

To Rose Marie, Melanie, and Joan—
three very special people in my life.

A saying or an aphorism is a concise observation on life.
If it is valid, it can be immensely helpful to others.

The sayings in this book represent observations Dr. Ben
Weininger and I have made over a period of several decades.
A few years ago, however, we began writing our insights down,
first in chapter form, then reducing them to short essays, next
to single pages, and finally hitting on the present aphoristic
style.

Dr. Ben, as he is affectionately called by many, was especially
gifted for this task. As my teacher and closest friend he frequently impressed me with the clarity, conciseness, and sim-
plicity of his expression. He is the only psychiatrist I can
understand. He is one of the most creative and profoundly
insightful persons of our era and through his recent writing
finally is achieving the recognition he richly deserves.

Dr. Ben and I enjoyed doing this book together. We learned
a good deal in the process. I hope you, the reader, will have a
similar experience and find it enjoyably enlightening.

May it help deepen your insights and possibly motivate you
to create your own aphorisms. Who knows? Maybe someday
you will be joining Lucy, Ben, and me in the booth of the 5¢
psychiatrist.

Meanwhile, as my friend Louise Lasker used to say, "Remember, life by the yard is hard—but life by the inch is a cinch."

Henry Rabin

IN MEMORIAM
Hugh Woodworth

A person of integrity who devoted his life to comprehending the nature of man and to articulating that understanding. His books are *The Nature and Technique of Understanding*, a study in semantics, *Sanity Unheard Of: Zen, the Turn Toward Life*; and a last, yet unpublished book, *The Biological Basis of the Soul*, from which the following is taken:

"It is true that on the negative side a species can meet devolution or extinction, but on the positive side there would appear to be *no limitation of consciousness*. It is a startling thought. It may well be that consciousness is the dominating factor in evolution and in the universe, and the physical body merely its handmaiden—which, if true, certainly should not deprecate the body, but would rather sanctify and elevate it, since it is through the body, its senses and nervous system, that so much consciousness is born."

Have every emotion,
hang onto none.

If everyone
could go to someone to talk to
an interested silent listener
or a counselor
for Five Cents,
we would have a better world
to live in. —Charles Schulz

To learn to love the many —
love the one.
To learn to love the one —
love the many.

Every body needs a hug.

Compromise
without resentment
is the key
to living together.

If we can live without each other,
we can live together.

It's good
to base your actions
on probability
rather than possibility.

We don't know
what we should be
really worrying about.
So why worry?

We don't see things as they are,
but as we are.

I am the way I feel,
not the way I appear.

We would be better able
to cope with everyday existence
if we genuinely perceived
that living is difficult —
that living
by its very nature
is a constant challenge.

Hanging on to anything—
in the outer
or the inner world—
is the bottleneck
in human growth.

You can't hate
your mother
and love
your husband.

If you want to do something
and are uncertain,
wait—
and wait and wait
until the desire passes.

14

Act as though you're in love and you may find yourself in love.

Life resides
in our
everyday actions.

Indecision
is a form of dependency:
You are waiting for somebody
to give you an answer.

Learn to love and love to learn.

It is difficult
to improve ourselves.
The best
that most of us can do
is to cast light
on the way we are.

Pay attention
to your friend's feelings;
it is a cure for self-centeredness.

Jealousy is
the pain or resentment
of being number two.

Three-fourths
of the trouble
that happens to us
is of our own creation;
one-fourth
is beyond our control.

Ailments
are
inverted
anxiety.

Even the "normal"
tend to overprotect themselves.

17

Learn,
live,
love,
laugh,
and let go!

Permit yourself
to be imperfect
and
give yourself license
to be what you are.

I once bought a lifetime pen—
I lost it in two weeks.

Happiness
can be achieved
only through a relationship
with all of life—
through other people, through work,
through your relationship with nature,
through your relationship
with the universe.

Imagine that the worst thing you fear has already happened, then you will have a sense of freedom from fear.

—Hugh Woodworth

You achieve mental health not by going after anything, but by being aware of the illusory nature of our strivings.

When I don't know how I feel, I ask my body.

Learn to play with psychological ideas, rather than making work of it.

The feeling of being insecure
is a real one;
our feeling
of being in a safe position
is an illusion.

Life
consists of taking risks,
sticking your neck out,
exposing yourself,
shedding your armor,
being unprotected,
not knowing the outcome,
making a move with uncertain results.

To grow,
risk.

Most of us assume
that people need each other
more and more.
It is only
in needing each other
less and less
that affection and love can grow.

The lesson
of the first part of life
is to find a secure relationship;
the lesson of the second half
is to realize
there is no secure relationship.

Going the second mile
is an attitude of mind—
a willingness
to do more
than the situation requires.
Learn to go the second mile genuinely.
Therein lies the greatest possibility
for personal fulfillment
that I have encountered
in the whole field
of personal psychology.

Those who value relationship
more than their hurt pride
make up sooner.

We need to learn to lose
to the other person
gracefully
and
without resentment.

When you come to an impasse and
see that you cannot resolve a certain
inner conflict, then the fruitless struggle
stops and there is a sense of wholeness.

24

Nobody
will give you
freedom —
you need to take it.

If you must compare yourself
to others,
compare yourself
to what you once were.

Learn to be
a loving and compassionate person.
This is the goal of life —
this is the direction.

Don't spend all your life
trying to get milk
from a bull.

We must have the courage
to allow
a little disorder
in our lives.

Everything that happens
can be a learning happening.

Of achievement,
we have enough!
Of kindness,
we must learn more.

Fulfilling your potential
as a human being,
not as an achiever,
is the objective.

We approach new life with past hurts.

Life has no age.
It contains
all of the past and future
in the Eternal Now.

Blessed is he
who lives
in the Eternal Now.
even for a while.

It is easier to let go of the past when
there is contact with another.

I can't know what my future holds.
I don't need to know.
When I do know, it becomes boring.

If you feel
you are young
or feel you are old,
you've lost touch
with your life source.

Too often
we allow our behavior
to be based on simple fears:
fear of losing money,
fear of losing a mate;
fear of losing health;
or fear of losing face.

Some deprivation
from time to time
renews our senses
and our spirit.

29

What you
resist,
persists.

Depressive reactions
often result
from giving yourself
impossible tasks to achieve.

After some frustration,
a heightened awareness.
After severe frustration,
a lowered awareness.

If you lack trust
in the mixed motives of others,
it is your purer motives
that can motivate them.

I am one—
I am two—
I am three.
One, two, three, love.

When I am with you, I am with you.
When I am not with you, I am not
with you.

If I am fully with you,
my self
is absent.

When I'm silently aware
of your presence,
that is relationship.

I am what I am.
But unfortunately
and unknowingly
I condemn what I am.

An objective of therapy
is to learn
to be easier
on yourself and on others.

Nothing negative
that you say about yourself
has any conviction
when I see
that you are really beautiful.

Ultimately, health is having faith in
another human being—and most of
all, in yourself.

32

Anxiety causes people to have selective inattention. It doesn't allow them to see the obvious.

You are not
ugly or bad —
you *feel* ugly or bad.

Anger is our response when we condemn what is.

Most of us
are more interested
in proving that we're right
than in what is best for ourselves
or our relationships with others.

An hour a day spent without purpose
has some surprises.

        Intervals of lying fallow —
        idleness —
        allow us
        to gain a perspective.

If a young person
feels like idling away
his time,
he is also learning something
about living
that may not be immediately apparent
to others.

        If you don't know what to do
        after graduation,
        wait and see what happens.

Relaxed attention
is based on interest and curiosity.
Forced attention and concentration
are based on fear.

Many people use their eyes to see
whether other people approve and
their ears, to learn whether other people like to hear them.

Being overly involved with people
and more people,
we lose the sense of aloneness.

In eating too much food
we lose the real sense of hunger.

Neurosis
is the lack of courage
to do
what common sense dictates.

If neurosis is the absence of courage,
sometimes healthiness is the courage
to admit its absence.

Heaven and hell
are actually the same place.
It's only our attitude
that makes them seem different.

36

If you are open to love and you are able to receive and give love and you are able to work, what else is there?

Life is not humorous, but there is humor in everything.

I usually relate to the healthy part of a person no matter how small it may be.

Your self-opinion often is often a reflection of what others think of you.

I found my wife's voice too loud. She married another who found it too soft.

Complete togetherness
or no togetherness at all
are not the only alternatives.

When I am close to another, the kind
of person I am is revealed.

The person who has "a need to be
close to only one" is prone to easy
anger.

When you are clinging—be aware.

We need to learn
to make molehills
out of molehills.
        —Elizabeth Mann Borghese

More important than the answer to a question is the questioning itself. It wakes us up and gives us perspective.

Making a commitment is one way to free yourself—your mind is no longer indecisive.

If you're kindly, you can be critical.

40

It is said: The sages are not in paradise, but paradise is in the sages. The truth is that paradise is in us all, but only the sages know it.

The superfluous word
is the one
that causes the trouble.

The pride image is the key to all hurt.
It should be the key question in all
human relationships.

You don't have to change yourself,
but be aware of trying to force change
on others.

The objective of life
is simple:
It's to be
a loving person.

The first step to freedom is to reject absolute rules. They are part of the tyranny of the should.

Anyone who cares for you
can be your therapist.

We keep making the same mistakes over and over until we learn something about the nature of love.

Most of our noisy activities are compulsive escapes from being silent and alone because we do not know how to enjoy being silent and alone.

Talk,
and you maintain distance;
be silent,
and you are close.

Compulsive talking is a way of expres-
sing the fear of intimacy.

Neurotic behavior is quite predictable.
Healthy behavior is unpredictable.
                              —Carl Rogers

What you are looking for
you already have.
What you don't have
isn't worth looking for.

When you have a relationship with someone do not try to change him. Facilitate his learning and changing.

Your parents can be your friends when you learn to drop them as parents.

You can be a child more
if you need to be one less.

45

If you are afraid
that your pre-teenager
is going to give you trouble
as an adolescent,
then share your fears and expectations
with other parents
who have similar fears.

Fears about
your teenage children's development
is lack of trust
in your own growth.

Most young people's problems
are transient.

Fortunate is the person
who allows himself
to respond appropriately.

Feelings alone
are not enough.
Behavior
needs to be checked
by reason.

Awareness of your reactions
will reveal
whether your fixed images or beliefs
are being threatened.

The breast and the ego
are the last to go.

We may be alone—
but if we do not seek to "escape,"
we are not lonely.

Ultimately,
the only thing people are afraid of
psychologically
is losing face—
this truth
must be ever discovered anew.

You may need six meals a day
or may need two,
but three are not essential.

One who has a deep need
for the approval of only one,
goes from one
to one
to one.

If you feel hate, fear or anger
when you meet someone,
it may be that he is expecting
you to feel that way about him.
Surprise him!

Hanging on to one's feelings
is an important cause of
self-created suffering.

Am I loved?
Am I worthy?
Am I making an important
contribution?
Am I attractive?
If you ask these questions, the answer
comes up No.

Too often we cloud our vision with mental pictures of what we think we should be like or what others should be.

When you are open to your own feelings, then you are more sensitive in your interactions with the feelings of others.

Be sensitive as to whether the other person's feelings are open or closed to you. It will serve as a guide in your relationship.

Resentment
ties me to you.
Caring and loving
free me from you.

A son becomes free
of the father
when he cares
for the father.

To be free of another, don't drop the
person, drop the emotional reactions.

If you do whatever is at hand well, you will also do the next thing well.

"Never" or "always" are misperceptions.

If we stop fussing about time, we might get a feeling of the timeless.

If pain feels like it will last forever, it is because of our fears.

If I'm on the right track more than half the time, I'm lucky.

Anger gives you the feeling of power.
Hurt leaves one feeling vulnerable.

Power is the easier one;
Being vulnerable is the harder one.

Live more during the day;
sleep better at night.

If you are overly concerned with your body image, then you are not sufficiently aware of your feelings.

I know less and see farther.

It's better generally to move in dangerous and uncharted areas than to move and stagnate forever in safe and familiar places.

If just
one person
has courage,
then there is hope
for the world.

The vision of a better world is our guide to it.

The less secretive,
the more healthy.

If we are kinder to ourselves,
we will be kinder to others.

If you are tired of getting repeatedly
beaten down, take a second and third
look at what's happening. You may be
setting yourself up.

Be honest with yourself but tactful
with others.

I lost my glasses and my day was ru-
ined. My friend lost his and bought
another pair.

Seriousness with an element of play
gives me perspective.

We need
a little bit of sunshine,
a little bit of bread,
and a little bit of companionship.
The rest is all a bonus.

People who live by love—live.

I waste time and energy maintaining
an *image* of being a good
Worker,
Marital partner,
Friend,
Parent,
Child,
Lover.
I am more when I am what I am.
And I may truly be all of those.

Look for the small fears — the big fears
are too difficult to cope with at first.

When we try to escape
from our small fears,
they become
big fears.

Mental health is achieved, at least in
part, by awareness of the false nature
of many of our strivings.

Keep your heart open
always,
and your door closed
sometimes.

When you are ready to learn, a teacher will appear.

When I describe what I'm learning, others say I'm teaching.

If you want to be a champion, you must abandon the coach.

— John Landy

Create like a God . . .
Work like a slave.

— Brancusi

Without risk and failure there is no new learning.

The door to learning and love opens when we see and hear without fear.

Your older sister picks on you because she is interested in you.

Directions can only be hinted at; the person must do the walking.

Every child needs a lap.

> With children,
> the secret is
> to be sensitive
> to any need or opportunity
> for communication.

Children need to feel like an only child
from time to time.

When your children don't need you
any longer, it means you've done your
job.

A good parent is one who doesn't try to be a good parent but one who is available when needed.

Fear and lack of trust in children's capacity to grow causes rebellion.

A hyperactive child does better in a structured environment.

Siblings acquire different interests to diminish their rivalry.

We are born dependent and die dependent.

Independence is an illusion. When I'm independent I isolate myself.

When I am self-reliant I include you. I am interdependent.

If you're alive and aware,
you're perfect.
Celebrate your perfection!
Show your love to someone.

The need for approval is so deep that it blocks the important perception that others are seeking our approval as well.

People who assume the approval of others have an easier time living together.

Being uninvolved in the long run is more destructive than the pain of involvement.

— Mark Braumlich

The less closeness a person enjoys, the more obsessive he becomes.

Fear cannot exist in the present.

The two most basic fears? The fear of dying—and the fear of living.

If you really care for your child,
whatever you do won't traumatize him.

The more I push the child
away from me,
the more he clings to me.
Hold the child on your lap
with full attention.
He will let you go.

Don't expect adult responses from im-
mature children.

A child adapts differently
to each parent
if one parent feels
more comfortable with discipline
and the other with permissiveness.

One parent is sufficient
for a child's needs
if the parent doesn't feel sorry
for herself or himself
because there is no partner.

Two parents
are better than one.
Three or four
neighboring parents
are better than two.

If we learn to be whole, the chances of being healthy are improved.

My body may be ill and dying but in spirit I can be whole.

My body can be healthy and my spirit can be divided.

Sick bodies can be treated by doctors, but divided souls interfere with the body healing.

Love is a cosmic force that comes to you and exists between you and another. You do not own it.

—Martin Buber

Being in love is a state of consciousness in which it is you that feels beautiful and you attribute it to your beloved.

An awareness of the sequence of events in relationships contains much of what is in interpersonal psychiatry.

—Harry Stack Sullivan

If you are elated or depressed, it is helpful to be aware of what went on before.

Some maximize pain because of fear of the unknown. Some minimize pain because their image is threatened.

An adult suffering the loss of love is also really suffering the loss of face.

Unless you are ill, *drift into your diet,* give yourself a year or so. Don't *go on* a diet, it's not good for you to keep on failing.

You have to shift some of your interest from solving your work problems to trying to solve some love problems.

When you love what you do, success is a by-product.

Leave when you leave.

"Honor thy father and mother." You honor your father and mother most when you grow up yourself.

A married person or a human being who happens to be married—which will you be?

Affection and tenderness with or without sex are freeing.

My body has an age, but I don't.

Aging creatively begins in childhood.

If I'm in a hurry, I take off my watch.

Be a willow tree instead of an oak.

If a baby is genuinely wanted,
his basic trust remains
even with many traumas.

A baby picks up your anxious feeling.
Knowledge about baby care
doesn't hide the feelings.

Discipline or permissiveness —
a child adapts to a either
or both
if there is real parental interest.

When a child is not wanted,
neglect is better than discipline.
An unwanted child who is disciplined
learns to hate.

Sustained conflict between the parents,
conscious and subconscious,
interferes with the child's experience
of a sense of wholeness.

Complaining degrades the complainer and overburdens the listener.

You cannot have freedom if you are frequently angry, for you are giving too much of your own power to another person.

Be aware of the condemning tendencies within yourself and others will see you as accepting them unconditionally.

Resentment
is more binding
than love.

Hate is a product of the unfulfilled life.
—Erich Fromm

Work or activity
is needed
for our spirit
as well as for our muscles.

Just be your symptom;
don't try to get rid of it.
In a sense,
love the symptom.

Watch your disturbed feelings;
don't escape or brush right over them,
but give them your attention
for a while.

When you relinquish a false hope,
there is a sense of freedom.

We need
a psychological
friendship in which
we are not afraid
to reveal ourselves.

The message of most great spiritual
teachers is simply, "Learn to stand on
your own two feet."

Hurt is real—all else
is rationalization
to avoid the pain.

81

My lover
has as many faces
as I have moods.

A lover is aware
of his beloved—
he is not a sex athlete.

Jealousy means a certain lust for living and involvement and, like all emotions, is a source of life energy.

Jealousy becomes a hazard only if it
drags on and on.

To some of us, everyone is an authority figure.

Confessional dependence is the need to tell mother everything.

We need to understand ourselves in order to be less self-centered.

I remember in order to forget.

Who am I that you ask me to accept you?

There are two I's.
The small *i* (ego) can be described;
the eternal *I* is unique and cannot be described.

Fixed ideas and beliefs
create
your reactive problem emotions.

Discouragement
is not a sign
of hopelessness
but a signal
that you are still clinging
to a concealed false hope.

A person of high intelligence
often doesn't find
the right work for himself
until he is older.

A profession without dedication
becomes routine work.

In the future
more people will create and invent
their own work
by pursuing what interests them.
Why wait?

I don't want from people what they can't give.

It's not the problem that matters, it's your attitude toward it.

A spiritual person is dependent on everyone, and therefore dependent on no one.

An Hasidic sage always carried two notes in his pocket. One read, "For me alone was the universe created." The other, "Dust and ashes art thou."

Confidence
is the ability
to find love
in many places.

To avoid pain, some people will go
through any torture.

A most extraordinary feat?
To be an ordinary person.

The secret of aging is
to be more and more content
with less and less.

Two lovers make a courtship but not necessarily a marriage.

It takes three to make a marriage: He, she, and the community.

One of the functions of marriage is to start growing again at the point where you left off as a child.

Marriage is for learning about yourself and others.

Many a couple are in a "hide-and-go-seek" relationship—with one always hiding and the other forever seeking.

If you want to dislike a person—you will easily find a host of justifiable reasons.

When I give,
I give myself.

All real living is meeting.
—Martin Buber

It is easier
to feel guilty over trivia
than our failure
to improve the world
in some small way.

Weaning is an intermittent life-long process. Death is the final weaning.

The present problem will go away. It's your next problem that's your main concern.

Meditation is free association around a problem without pressing for a solution.

Learn to take a vacation without guilt feelings.

A person will get along with you
in the same way he got along
with his parent.

Work through the unresolved problems
with your father or mother
before you commit yourself
to a "life-long" relationship
with another.

If marriages were tentative, they would
last longer.

When we are angry often we are concealing our hurt. When we are anxious often we are concealing our rage.

Anger is one way
of getting control
when you are afraid
of being vulnerable,
but
to allow yourself
to be vulnerable
opens the way
to affection
and tenderness.

'Think fat' —
'Think thin' —
Think neither.

A cat alone
does very well
as long as the kittens
have playmates.

                    The fear of humiliation
                    makes slaves of us all.

The "sergeant" gets total attention,
and gets hated in the process.

We are too much self-preoccupied. Be aware of how much time each day you are self-concerned.

If you are totally interested in a person, you break out of a shell.

I need to stop fighting myself.
I need a vacation.

The two hardest things for a human being to give up — dependence on people, especially mother figures, and the hardest of all, pride.

The most commonly used and the least effective escape from the pain of conflict in a relationship is the attempt to change your partner.

Who should make up first? The one who sees that holding back hurts him more than his partner.

Learn to be fully present,
even if
the other is not.
You might
receive a response.

Too often we look at adult relations through child's eyes.

When you feel angry at your children because they don't write — call them.

Is your daughter more important or is it some principle in your mind?

Which is more important: letting your child explore or doing the housework?

The main problem of parents is that self-interest is greater than interest in children.

Sharing children while they are young with a community of friends for week-ends, for overnights, or even just for meals allows them to see a variety of family styles, rather than only one view.

First feed the animals,
then the children,
then yourselves.
   —from the Talmud

When you blame yourself or another person, you are trying to maintain an image of yourself.

God can only help those who do not justify their behavior.

—Hasidic saying

Talk from personal experience, then you will be authentic.

Being aware of the center of gravity of your body creates a harmony between body and mind

If I'm fearful—
If I'm angry—
If I'm jealous—
If I'm coy—
If I feel dependent— the feelings
I have are not my problems.
My *attitudes*
toward these feelings
are
my *psychological problems*.

The door
to learning and love
opens
when we see and hear
without fear.

We go through life accentuating slights and ignoring the many kindnesses of life.

Maintain a balance between love and work and play; some of us dissipate too much energy on one or the other.

Sometimes I'm so clear, I realize how great my confusion really is.

—D.H.

It is not the vulnerability to another that is destructive. It is the possessive attachment.

Depending on only the one breeds hostility.

Learn to love everyone, even your husband or wife.

Relationship conflicts are based on being too much married, too much mutual clinging.

We keep only that which we set free.
—Chinese origin

Being involved is our teacher.

During moments when I'm fully awake, my past doesn't function.

Without anticipation and without expectation, we are fully in the Now.

When I'm fully in the Now, I'm not concerned as to how I feel about myself.

One life is long enough to complete one's Karma. Reincarnation now.

Fear concerns the future
and the past,
In the eternal Now,
there is no fear.

Feeling hurt without trying to escape or justify that reality opens the door to your heart.

When I make a mistake, I can make a mental correction. I do not need to condemn myself.

You accept the "shoulds" and the "oughts" imposed by others to avoid living through your feelings.

If you are elated or depressed, it is helpful to be aware of everything that went before.

An awareness of the sequence of events is much of what psychiatry is.

The absence of the feeling of community creates the need for psychotherapy.

We need to be sometimes alone and sometimes together. We're afraid of distance, and also afraid of close relations. We run from distance to relations and then from relations to distance.

We need to learn
to choose:
Sometimes distance,
and sometimes relations
without fear.

Without distance there is no dialogue between the two.

—Martin Buber

We are born self-centered—all our basic needs must be met before we can smile—being held securely, being touched, being warm, being fed, *being wanted,* being rested.

There is a difference
between being
self-centered,
which is unhealthy,
and being centered
in one's self,
which is being in touch
with the essence
of one's being.

Sexual intercourse is not an instinct in the human being. It is the desire for closeness and contact that is instinctive.

Sexual wishes are desires for closeness, not necessarily for intercourse.

A man places too much pride in the activities of his penis. A woman places too much pride in whether she has an orgasm or not.

Anxiety and depression make one more vulnerable to being in love.

When I'm in love, my unresolved problems from childhood surface— jealousy, possessiveness, resentment, self-blaming, blaming others. When we resolve these childhood feelings, we learn to love and care for the other person.

Lovers find indifference more difficult to handle than emotional outbursts.

Laughter is one way towards health and enlightenment.

If you don't take yourself too seriously, others will take you more seriously.

I asked a friend when she began to laugh. She said, "I began to laugh when my life was in a state of total disaster."

You need to find a friend
with whom you can laugh.
It becomes contagious.

Anxiety, depression, and a sense of failing make one more susceptible to being twice born.

It is a state of consciousness in which you feel whole—a sense of delight—a sense of contact with the life force of the universe. We are all brothers and sisters and have one father.

It is usually triggered by another person who gives you the feeling of being unconditionally accepted.

There is a hidden negative aspect to being twice born. The unconscious unresolved problems from the past remain and are unrecognized. This leads to a need to convert others.

We are made
in the image of God.
The infant
is nobly born.

Whenever you're disturbed, nine times out of ten you'll find that an image of yourself has been knocked down.

The creative energy you use
in maintaining and
in rebuilding your image
can be put to better use if it
goes into projecting
your real self.

We can learn to be whole by saying what we mean and doing what we say.
—Martin Buber

Without some emotional separation, distance, or an emotional divorce happening, the problematic relationship can only be patched up—not made whole.

A legal divorce
is often followed
by years of resentment and distrust
because the marriage
has never really
ended.

A psychological and emotional divorce
before legal divorce is undertaken
is good for all in the family.

The only constructive way of breaking up a marriage is to learn how to become friends.

Let the children have a say with whom they want to live. Contrary to general opinion, separating the children is often beneficial for all people involved.

In many circumstances mild depression is a healthy response.

Moderate depression may conceal rage directed against oneself because of fear of directing the rage at someone else.

Chronic depression often has a chemical as well as a psychological base. Chemical as well as psychological help may be necessary. Do not blame yourself.

When I'm afraid of going along with change, I'm afraid of dying—but I haven't lived, either.

Every pain
is a miniature
of the great pain—
the fear of dying.

The process of dying itself is painless.

Fear aggravates pain. Pain often is a way of saying something else, such as, "I want support and closeness."

When you are in pain, see how much of it is fear. When you discover the fear, you can better cope with the pain.

It is the personality of the healer that facilitates the healing, not a theory of personality.

If there is faith in the healer, healing takes place.

Remember that a child can be traumatized by being repeatedly humiliated.

In the adult, the reverse is true—the adult needs to take risks in situations in which the image of himself might be embarrassed or humiliated.

When we think that happiness will come through another person, we create the occasion for mutual hurting.

We maintain our inner conflicts to avoid conflict with our family, friends, and the social environment. We create a facade of peace at the expense of inner turmoil.

We have more than the two options of inner or outer conflict. When we resolve our inner conflicts through spiritual relationships with others, we can feel whole.

As we age and have more and more losses in the outer world, we need to look into our inner world, our spiritual center that connects us with all of life.

A listening friend can help us find this inner spiritual community or communion.

You have achieved
the ultimate
when you feel
that you are part
of the life force
of the universe.
and you have learned
to love the one,
the many,
and yourself.